# Living Silence

## Tuning in and Practising

First printed in Germany (in German) 2003

www.herder.de
ISBN – 13: 978-3-451-05293-4
ISBN – 10: 3-451-05293-8
First published in English 2013

www.oxfordzencentre.org.uk



Matador
9 Priory Business Park
Kibworth Beauchamp
Leicestershire LE8 0RX, UK
Tel: (+44) 116 279 2299
Fax: (+44) 116 279 2277
Email: books@troubador.co.uk
Web: www.troubador.co.uk/matador

ISBN 978 1783062 720

British Library Cataloguing in Publication Data.
A catalogue record for this book is available from the British Library.

Printed and bound in the UK by TJ International, Padstow, Cornwall

**Matador** is an imprint of Troubador Publishing Ltd

Silvia Ostertag

# Living Silence

## Tuning in and Practising

Translated from the German by

Susanne Ehrhardt and Wendy R. Tyndale

# CONTENTS

# TRANSLATORS' NOTE

Silvia Ostertag was greatly esteemed by the many practitioners of Zen at the Oxford Zen Centre who had an opportunity to spend time with her. It was therefore not surprising that the teacher of the Centre, John Gaynor, looked for someone to translate her book *Lebendige Stille*, into English. We were glad to accept the task.

In the course of our work, we received much encouragement and skilled help from Helga Gramlich, a German Zen practitioner and close friend of the Ostertag family, and from Johanna Ostertag, the author's daughter.

Silvia Ostertag was trying to convey experiences that are almost impossible to put into language, and her German is often idiosyncratic in its density, as well as being expressive and poetic. Our aim has been to remain as close to the original as possible while at the same time doing our best to give the English reader a flavour of the beauty of her writing.

We have sometimes wrestled to find the nearest English equivalent of certain words and phrases, but we have always enjoyed doing it and feel that our own understanding has deepened through the exceptionally careful reading that translation demands.

Our warmest thanks are due to Sandy Bharat, who has kindly given her time and skills to prepare the manuscript for publication and to Vanessa for her photograph on the front cover.

Susanne Ehrhardt and Wendy Tyndale
Oxford, June 2013

# PREFACE

There is no road to the place where we have always been. There is no outside without an inside, no up without a down. But our ego prevents us from seeing the complete picture, from experiencing unity. It separates, distinguishes and specifies. This is its role, this makes us human. But it dominates us. It prevents us from seeing the whole. It is as if someone holding a stick in his hand can only see one end of it.

Because of this, we need guidance, someone to accompany us who has been there before, who has experienced oneness and knows how to get there. Guidance which can lead us beyond the ego's limitations.

It is in exactly this sense that Silvia Ostertag's book can accompany us on the way. Along this way are many traps we may stumble into: beautiful places where we would like to linger, summits which trick us into believing we have reached the goal. On the spiritual path, too, our ego plies the counterfeit wares it does not want to give up. Beyond the personal consciousness there are also snares to entangle you.

This book is a guide, like Ariadne's thread which led Theseus through the labyrinth. Like a compass, it allows you to check whether you are heading in the right direction.

Willigis Jäger

## AUTHOR'S THANKS

I would like to thank all those who have ever practised sitting in silence with me, to whom I have spoken words of orientation like the ones to be found in this little book.

I thank my friend Dr. Wolf Büntig who, when we gave courses together, prompted me to write down and publish what I had said about practising.

I thank my teachers Karlfried Graf Dürkheim and Willigis Jäger. Their inspiration and patience have always encouraged me to remain true to my practice.

I thank my husband Albrecht for his careful revision of the manuscript and for his very helpful advice on the choice of the texts.

I thank Albrecht, our son Dominik, our daughter Johanna and all those closest to me for being my teachers day by day.

I thank stone, plant, animal and human being for unceasingly manifesting the essential.

# INTRODUCTION

## REMEMBERING SILENCE

Most people have had an experience of silence – in fact probably everyone, though it is impossible to verify that, so let us say most. If you take time to look back, you will know that you have experienced silence as something special, something good, something difficult to describe.

If you take time to remember. Not much time is needed. It is enough to allow yourself a moment's silence – now, for example – without seeking or wanting anything; just letting yourself be silent, open to the possibility that a memory of silence may surface in this being silent. Then most people remember.

It may be that the moment occurs at the end of a working day, when the noise of a pneumatic drill suddenly stops. As if a great wave of silence were descending over the place which only a moment ago was vibrating with the din, spreading over the whole city and at the same time into every cell of your body.

Or maybe you remember the silence that you perceived at some point for the first time between two notes, even though you had heard the piece of music many times before. All at once this silence, where until then there was only a pause.

Or it could be the memory of a moment of silence in a conversation. A moment at which everything was said, even the unsayable. Or the memory of an old church in which you once sat alone in the half darkness and the silence made you forget where you were sitting.

Or it may be that you remember a walk in the woods. You remember how you walked into a wood and stood still every now and then, listening.

The gentle murmur of the wind in the trees. The faint rustling in the undergrowth. The creaking of a branch. Birdsong. You are silent and listen. Sometimes there is nothing to hear. No sound. 'No sound' is not nothing, although 'no sound' is not anything either.

Silence. Far and wide. Silence leads us to perceive the far and wide. No sound. Neither outside nor inside. In this 'no-sound' there is neither outside nor inside.

Although nothing moves, although there is nothing to hear, everything is there. If, in all this silence, you hold your breath for a moment, it is still breathing.
'Not-breathing' breathes. Like the trees and the wind.
And like me.
Living silence.

There – there was that rustling again. And yet nothing has been interrupted. The squawk of a bird – as if it belonged to the silence. For a moment you realise that nothing can disturb this silence.

And when you walk on, your own footsteps also seem for a while to be completely part of the silence. As if steps were nothing but silence.
But at some point you began to think about this and that and came out of the wood and left the silence too. You simply forgot about it, you do not know how it happened.

Everything is ordinary again.
Yes, something was out of the ordinary.

In your memory it is there again, just there. Even though you are not standing in the wood. It was there again – the silence. Without the wood. Without the rustling. Without anything.

Silence is there as soon as you remember silence.
And silence is there as soon as you listen for silence.

## IT IS ENOUGH TO LISTEN FOR THE SILENCE

It is enough to listen for the silence.
To do so, you do not need to fly to the desert or sit in an old church. Nor do you need to go into the woods.

Whenever you want to, you can enter the silence inside yourself.
There, there is a place like a quiet wood.
There, there is no word – far and wide.

When you have spent a while there with yourself in the silence, you will forget the silence again – just as when you came out of the woods. Nevertheless, having been in the silence bears fruit. Just as, if you reflect on it, every tiny experience of silence has an effect, for a short time anyway.

## THE EFFECT TRANSFORMS

The effect transforms. It may transform only very faintly, but still it transforms – somehow as if your ears unintentionally hear something in what they are listening to that cannot be heard with the ears: in everything, in every single sound or noise. As if your eyes see something in what they are looking at that cannot be seen with the eyes. In everything, in the tree, in the window frame, in the dog, in the human face.

And you know or feel that you are moved or stirred by precisely that which your senses and reason cannot grasp. What stirs you is this indescribable thing itself, through which you feel connected with everything in a unique way; as if you were one with every sound and every object and every living creature, one with a single indescribable Self.

In this state of mind, how could you not wish every creature well? How could you not be of good will? How could you, if you remained in this state of mind.

But we do not remain there. Whether we are only fleetingly touched by such an experience or whether we have been shaken to the core by it, this state of mind will not hold out against our all too habitual thoughts and feelings where we take to be true only what we perceive to be separate.

We reinforce this habitual way of seeing things day by day when we struggle against people and things, usually without noticing that we are doing so. And in order to compensate, every now and then we numb our senses and reason in some way or another, so as to make our separation bearable through the illusion that we are all one. But in this way we betray the one unifying element in the unique individual.

We are like this.

But we are not only like this. We sense, and sometimes unexpectedly experience the other reality. And in that experience we have the intuition of a sort of promise; the promise that we shall come to realise more and more who we really are. 'More and more' means allowing more and more space for the recognition of the essential reality and letting it work more and more in and through ourselves.

## SITTING IN SILENCE IS A WAY

Many people today follow this promise and set out on this path, seeking silence not only for a moment of relaxation, but in the sense of a practice.
When we have found such a practice we are still the same as ever. There are only a few saints, even though so many people have set off on the way.
Nevertheless, little by little something changes, or rather everything changes as soon as you take up a practice of silence.

You cannot make silence. Silence is there as soon as you do nothing. That is why in the practice of silence it is precisely a matter of doing 'as much of nothing as possible'.

This is easier said than done. But you can try – for a couple of minutes, right now, simply to do nothing, nothing at all. But now is unlikely to be the right moment. You are certain to have something more important to do just now, even if it is only to carry on reading. This is the first obstacle. There is almost always something more important to do than to do nothing, than merely to sit in silence.

If you want to commit yourself to the practice of sitting in silence you will do well to do it always at the same time. In the morning, for example, before breakfast, before your head is filled with a multiplicity of impressions and plans. But it can of course be in the evening or whenever you like, as long as it is at a time that you have set yourself, so that you cannot say that you have something more important to do just now.

If the practice of silence is to reach into all areas of our experience and action, to transform our everyday life, it will require a certain length of time. Twenty-five minutes is a good time. But this is only a guideline. Each minute of sitting in silence is more than not doing it at all. You will find out what length of time is good for you and also what kind of ritual you find appropriate to prepare for the practice – to light a candle, for example and turn towards the place of silence with a gesture of respect, a bow.

## INVITATION AND CHALLENGE

To sit in silence and really do nothing is no small challenge when you do not happen to be sitting in a beautiful old church or pausing in the woods listening.

Putting your hands in your lap is not too difficult. Nor is keeping your mouth shut for a while. But to still your feelings and silence your thoughts is a different matter. And for silence this is crucial. Not, of course, because it is bad to feel and think. It would be very good to be able to feel more deeply and think more clearly. It would be very good, too, not to be utterly taken over by emotions or distracted by involuntary thoughts but rather to create new thoughts out of a felt connectedness. Silence cleanses our emotions and thinking of compulsive identifications precisely because feeling and thinking remain quiet during this time.

It is for this reason that from time immemorial different spiritual traditions have developed helpful methods for sitting in silence. Common to them all is the aim of bringing your object-fixating consciousness into silence, of completely silencing your ordinary waking consciousness, so that when sitting you may find a connection with the foundation of your being deep in your soul and thereby wake up to your original oneness with all that is.

## POSTURE, BREATHING, COMPOSURE

Thus the recommendation common to all traditions is that we should concentrate our mind in a certain way. By focusing our attention on a single point, we free ourselves from multiple distractions. By staying with the One our attention itself gradually merges with it. When our object-fixating consciousness turns into silence, we reach a threshold where it is crucial not to slip into dozing or dreaming or to relapse into an unfocused state of mind but to allow ourselves to wake up to inner contemplation.

It is important, therefore, to pay attention to a well balanced sitting posture. Whether you sit on a chair, on a low bench or on a meditation cushion is not important in itself. However, it is easier to concentrate when you are in the closest possible contact with the ground. A relaxed and straight back is important, as is holding your head tall and free. This allows a free flow of breath.[1]

Alongside other possibilities for concentrating in the spirit of Zen or of contemplation, the movement of the breath is an excellent focus of attention. It is not important whether you count your breaths, or start with picturing the flow of your breath[2] or whether your attention simply follows your breath. When you make yourself aware of it, the flow of breath itself then affects your attention. It deepens and internalises your listening for silence.

Your attention flows more and more into your breath, your breathing fills your awareness more and more and your attention becomes more and more at one with your breath itself. More and more silence gathers around this process. Indeed, the process itself turns more and more into silence. More and more there is nothing but silence.

ONLY SILENCE

Then everything that is belongs to this silence, whether it is a sound, a feeling that arises or a thought.
Until this state of mind vanishes again, perhaps after a second, perhaps after a longer time – until it comes back, perhaps after a few minutes or after weeks – and then disappears again and comes back. Gradually the trail it leaves behind becomes more and more distinct so that in everyday life you are again and again unexpectedly reminded of the taste of silence. Then you wonder at the way in which situations and themes and problems gradually appear in a different light, as if an invincible benevolence were dawning in them.

## THE DRAMA OF INTEGRATION

Of course this integration of the experience of silence into one's whole personality and thus into everyday life will certainly, or at least usually, not happen smoothly or without drama, for what is waiting to change is no less than the understanding of everything and of one's self. Ever since growing out of the naivety of childhood, we have become used to interpreting all our perceptions and to giving them value and meaning according to our present level of knowledge and according to our capacity to make comparative judgments. We have become accustomed, too, to defining ourselves by an identification with our opinions: to believing that our opinions are who we are. I am someone who thinks and feels like this, who knows this, and means that.

The vision which develops out of an experience of silence cuts across this level of understanding and communication – in itself coherent – as a completely different dimension of knowing. In this dimension, each phenomenon reveals itself as itself, as whole and as the One itself.

For the ego-consciousness, which clings to an old way of seeing things, the dawn of a new vision is like a death. It defends itself and fights, until it is defeated and lets go and so discovers that is has been reborn from the centre of the cross in which the recognition of everything as different and the experience of everything as one permeate each other without contradiction. This is a long path of development which for many will lead through crises and distress, through valleys of darkness.

One of the difficulties is that the less you can accept yourself as you are, the harder it is to let go of yourself. In concrete terms for the practice, this means that the less reconciled you are with yourself, the harder it is to attain silence.
Or to put it the other way round, the more you allow yourself to be as you are, the easier it is to let go of your Me, the more you are transformed and the more stimulation others receive from you to transform themselves.

The difficulty with this difficulty is that you usually do not even know in what way or with regard to what you are unable to let go of yourself. For the bad things often lie on the shadow side of one's consciousness: envy, greed, hatred, fear, or whatever one might find unacceptable in oneself. But – thank goodness – in the practice of sitting, if you are serious about silence and if you do not talk yourself into believing in an effect before it happens in a different way than expected, you are sooner or later confronted with precisely these shadow characteristics.

You will experience such a confrontation as an act of purification. You will know that you are led by the promise and by the practice itself. And you will know whether and when you need stimulation from outside to guide you further.

## ABOUT THE PRACTICE AND THE TEXTS

Sitting in silence is a practice which can be carried out in principle on one's own, without any particular preconditions and in varying measure.

Those who want to commit themselves fully will do well eventually to join a practice group and above all to seek someone experienced to accompany them. A book cannot replace this sort of personal guidance. It can be, and aims to be, only an encouragement for the practice and a mirror for what has been experienced.

The division into chapters should not be understood as suggesting a structure for the practice. For each time you sit in silence it is a matter of arrival, of practice, of silence, of now and of a struggle with obstacle and shadow. The chapter 'What it is about' is not intended to be a theoretical sketch, but a way of getting attuned to silence.

Most of the texts originated in direct addresses to groups and were noted down and adapted for the written version afterwards. So as not to encroach upon the reader with the direct address 'you', I have chosen to use the less determined, but somewhat brittle and awkward infinitive for the introductory parts of the texts[3]. In this way I hope that it is possible to feel the scope for opening up to what might concern you and for feeling free to ignore what does not speak to you. And may you thus arrive in your very own silence.

---

1. See 'On Posture', page 104.
2. See 'Picturing the Flow of Breath', page 106.
3. Translators' note: We have translated these infinitives by a gerund and have actually used 'you' to translate the German *man*.

# ARRIVING

## IT IS ENOUGH TO LISTEN TO THE SILENCE

It is enough
to listen to the silence.
Silence comes to fetch us
where we have just been
with our thoughts and feelings.

It is enough
to listen to the silence.
Silence brings us
to where we are now,
right here,
into this room,
to this place,
this morning.

It is enough
to listen to the silence.
Silence embraces
what wants to become.
Whatever this day brings us,
is held,
and always has been,
in this silence
now.

It is enough
to listen to the silence.

## ARRIVING

Letting myself arrive
in this room, in this place,
in this body and in this posture,
in this form of mine.

Sensing how I am united with the ground, with the earth,
through my pelvis and my legs.
Sensing how this ground makes me aware of myself
just where I touch it,
so that the superfluous tension
which seemed needed to stay upright
dissolves by itself.

Sensing or intuiting
that there is space above my head.
With my mind, feeling my way into, growing into
this space above my head
without losing contact with the ground.

From this delicate upright tension,
perceiving the relation between one hand and the other,
being at home in the contact between my hands.
From here, from this being-at-home,
sensing the wide space around.

Arriving in my breath,
in-breath comes, I accept it – wherever from?
Out-breath goes, I let it go – wherever to?

Breath comes or goes.
My breathing breathes breath.
Breath breathes my breathing
in this in, in this out.

## YES

Letting yourself arrive here.
Noticing what you feel now.
Perhaps it is tiredness.
Or alertness.
Perhaps it is composure.
Or annoyance.
Anxiety
or joy.
Or excitement.
Rage
or sadness.
Or cheerfulness.

The still bodily posture
in which we always sit,
this still posture,
simply says yes to it,
just as posture.
Yes, this is how it is.
Yes, tiredness!
Yes, anxiety!
Yes, cheerfulness!
Yes, Yes.

As soon as the sober, silent Yes
spreads through and through,
this small Yes is itself
perfect silence.
This small Yes
is all-embracing warmth.
This Yes.

## BEING PRESENT

Letting your mind arrive at this place, at this spot.
Noticing your contact with the cushion, bench or chair
on which you are sitting,
and so feeling your relation with the ground, the earth.

Noticing the contact between the crown of your head and
the space above,
and so sensing the upward pull – skyward.
Sensing or intuiting also the space around you,
and so letting yourself arrive in relation to your
surroundings.

Noticing your breath, as it goes and comes,
and so letting yourself arrive within yourself.

Some people imagine
letting-themselves-arrive to be the preliminary practice
and that the real being-present will begin
after they have arrived.
Imagining this,
they never arrive in being-present.

For being-present is a continuous
letting-yourself-arrive
in relation to what is below and what is above,
to earth and sky,
in this relation
which is expressed
in our upright sitting posture – now.

And being-present is a continuous letting-yourself-arrive
in the movement between inside and outside,
in this movement of life
which is expressed
in our breath – now.

## BREATHING A SIGH OF RELIEF

Letting yourself arrive,
here, now.
Letting yourself sit
as though you were called
to sit, here, now.

Sitting
as though you were meant
to do nothing else
but to sit, here, now.

Now only this is meant.
Now I am meant.
Just as I am now.
Breathing out.
Breathing a sigh of relief.
Breathing.

## IT TAKES NO TIME

Some people think
that it always takes time
for the mind to arrive in the space of silence.

How about
simply dropping
this idea,
simply feeling
how you are sitting right now
in contact with the ground
and thus with the earth,
in this earth-contact
that knows neither here nor there.

Simply letting yourself feel
how you are sitting right now,
in contact with the space above your head
and thus with the sky,
in this sky-contact
which knows neither yesterday nor today.

Letting yourself feel
how you are sitting in contact
with your breathing as it occurs
and thus in contact with being
which knows neither life nor death.

Letting yourself sit
in this being
which is now,
here.

## VASTNESS

Simply immersing myself
again
in this vastness
which breathes
as though it were my breath.

Simply immersing myself
again
in this breath
which expands
as though it were the vastness.

Simply immersing myself
again
in this silence
which lives me.

## AGAIN, AT LAST

At last you are sitting again.
You have overcome all obstacles
in spite of the urgent matters
which seemed to call so loudly.

You have shut the door behind you
and are sitting again.
You have lighted the candle
and made a bow.

You have sat down
and carefully smoothed
the crease in your clothes.

You have joined your hands,
Your thumbs touch.
Your eyes are half closed.

At last you are sitting again.
Sitting.
Now.
Here.

## STRESS

Some people make everything stressful for themselves,
even sitting in silence.
They hardly appreciate
that now there is simply
this sitting still.
That in this practice
they may simply be.
That now there is this space
in which
they may be.
That there is time
in which
they may linger.
That there is this body
in which
they may dwell.
That there is this
flowing breath
through which
they may live.
That there is this silence
in which
they may keep silent.
That there is this silence
which they themselves
may simply be.

Some people hardly appreciate this.

## BETRAYAL

The day was so noisy.
Like a betrayal
of the morning's silence.

You were so noisy yourself.
Traitor to the silence.

But as soon as you
arrive once again
in the silence
you know
there is no betrayal.

Silence cannot
be betrayed
by anyone – ever.

As soon as you
arrive in the silence
you know that.

# PRACTISING

## BEGINNING

Now the practice of silence begins again,
just as it begins again
every morning.
This space
is here for me again,
just as every morning
space waits for me.

The flower, the candle
are here for me again,
just as something is ready for me
every morning.

Life is here for me again,
as it is every morning.

Now it begins again – with me.
It shall begin
with me playing my part.
With me being in it.
With my breathing.
With my silence.
With me.
With now.

## BEGINNER'S MIND

Let us practise with beginner's mind.
But what is beginner's mind?
It is a mind
which does not compare
because it does not know how things should be.

It is a mind
for which everything is perfectly new
because it does not know everything in advance.

It is a mind
which simply takes part
in what is happening right now.

What is happening right now?
Breath is flowing.

If I do not compare with previous breath
then this breath is completely new.
I myself am completely new
in this in and out,
I, beginner's mind.

Oh how different this situation or that encounter
might be
if only I could take part in them, just like this, with
beginner's mind!

Beginner's mind does not imagine
how something might be.
Beginner's mind is only here.
Here and now I am new.

## BREATH-ATTENTION

When attention
is focused on the breath
then the breath carries
the attention
as if of its own accord.

And although
the attention
rests
on the breath,
its feelers,
barely noticeable,
tend
to precede the breath
just a little.

## LOOKING THROUGH

Whatever
arises
as a so-called distraction,
whether thoughts, feeling or pain,

instead of fending it off
you could,
centred in your breath,
simply look through it
right into the silence.

## AS IF

More often than not, when you commit yourself
to this posture of sitting in silence
something is not yet right.

The silent posture does not match
the noise and restlessness
perceived within.

You are sitting as if.
As if you were quiet.
Some people try
to ignore this.
They pretend in their mind: 'as if'
and imagine silence.

The result of such sitting may then be
an 'as-if-composure'
in which you hide
instead of finding yourself.

It is better
to take note of the mismatch
between outward posture
and inner state.

Then the practice is
consciously to take up the still posture
with all the restlessness,
with all the inner noise,
until you gradually take part
in what silent-posture means and achieves.

## CHALLENGE

Some people automatically
feel stressed out
as soon as any demand is made on them.

As if it were wrong for life to make demands,
to challenge them to quit dull routine,
to challenge them to get in touch
with what is
and what wants to become.

But our life is nothing other
than this challenge.
The invitation to experience what is.
And, through experiencing, respond
to what wants to become of it.

Right now
my life is challenging me
out of sitting dully
into this breath,
into my lived response
to that which wants to become
of me and through me with this breath.

What is it like to breathe
when I allow demands to be made on me?

## BALANCE

No matter
with which personal method
of  concentration
we enter into the silent practice,
it is always a question of
finding a balance
between more actively
directing our attention
and more passively
allowing things to happen.

Sometimes, and perhaps more and more often,
a balance is found as if of its own accord.
Then there is hardly any more
shifting from here to there,
then there is
consummate action
at the same time as
complete letting go.

Then there is no more practising,
then there is shared accomplishing
from breath to breath
being breath
being silent,
being.

## RHYTHM

Practising is something natural.
Everything natural
follows a rhythm.
Rhythm arises
through change.
Change between
out and in,
high and low
or light and dark.

Why, when the practice is going well,
do we want it
to remain so?

Why, when the practice is going badly,
do we fear
it will remain so?

What stands still
is unnatural.

But the heart of rhythm
is the dimension
of the unchangeable.

The unchangeable
is the innermost part
of out and in,
the innermost part
of my high
and low.

## RUBBISH

You really want
to sit in silence
and simply
let your breath flow.
But then
some piece of rubbish
comes into your mind.
Such rubbish.
And more
rubbish.
Such rubbish.
Rubbish!
Ish
Sh

## IT IS ENOUGH

It is not a question of
practising particularly well.

It is enough
to practise.

It is not a question of
it being particularly silent.

It is enough
to enjoy even the tiniest little bit of silence
thoroughly.

## THOUGHT-STILLNESS

Thought-stillness
arises of its own accord,
the less you
fend off thoughts,
and the more you
savour
this breath
again and again.

## PRESSURE

Some people sit in silence
as if they
were under tremendous pressure.

When they notice it
they try
with all their might
to escape from
this pressure.

Why not try for once
to relax
your jaw just a little,
as if a smile
were allowed
to pass by some time?

## LETTING GO

You cannot
bring about letting go.
Letting go happens
most easily
when you admit to yourself
that you
cannot let go.

# WHAT IT IS ABOUT

## WHAT IT IS ABOUT

Some people do not
take the time
or claim the right
to sit
in silence
because, when all is said and done,
there are more important things in the world
than sitting around
on one's cushion.

Others do not claim
the right
to be engaged day by day
in the important things
to be done
in the world
without a basic practice of
working on themselves.

Therefore they sit down
in silence,
so that
day by day
silence
may transform them.

## NOT-THINKING

Some people doubt
whether a practice
in which thinking
is supposed to be silenced
can promote
mental development.

But in thought-silence
the capacity to think is
cleansed from the identification
with unconsciously adopted concepts
and from the obsessive enacting
of intellectual fantasies.

By participating in silence
we practice participation
in what has been thought and in thinking.

Taking part in thought, however,
is a precondition
for acting
creatively.

That is why some people seek
not-thinking in silence.

## WHO AM I

Engaging in a spiritual practice
is always prompted by the question: Who am I?

Sitting in silence is not meant as an opportunity
to reflect on this question.
Reflecting does not lead
you to realisation.

Sitting in silence is meant as an opportunity
to be in touch with this question right now.
Who am I in this breath?
In this out and in?

However, it is precisely with my questioning look
that I put my breath
at a distance.
I look here,
it breathes there.

But when,
starting with the question,
I enter in,
immerse myself thoroughly,
in this out and in,
then I forget the question.

Forget out and in,
forget who is sitting here
asking about herself.

Breathing being-forgotten
knows itself through me.

## PRESENCE

Sitting in silence leads into presence.
Presence is beyond opposites.
Beyond opposites means
to be and not to be
at the same time.

How can I
be
and
not be
in my breath?

The practice is only
to collect your senses
and enter into
this in-breath,
this out-breath.

To enter deeper and deeper
until you are one
with this in,
with this out.

There is no breath and no I
in the one-ness with breath.
No inside and no outside.
No something and no nothing.
In this neither-nor is presence,
breath by breath.

You do not have to understand it.
It is enough
to experience it.

You do not have to
seek the experience.

It is enough
to enter into
this breathing in,
this breathing out.
Now and now.

## INNER SELF

Sitting in silence is a practice
for looking into your inner self.
Some people
search for the inner self
inside their skin
or inside their feelings
or thoughts.

The inner self is not bound by space.
It extends
as far as the horizon.

When that becomes true for someone
their breath goes out and in
on the horizon.

## LETTING BE

Sitting in silence means
letting yourself be.
Letting yourself be, here,
in this place,
in this room,
in this body,
in this breath.
Letting yourself be.

Sitting in silence means
letting yourself be.
Letting yourself be
as you are,
as you have become,
strong and weak,
good and bad.
Letting yourself be
as you are just now, here.

Sitting in silence means
letting yourself be.
Leaving yourself to being.
To being
which becomes and becomes
according to the law
which creates itself.

Leaving yourself to being
which creates you
as its Now,
just like this,
just here.

## GOD SLEEPS IN THE STONES

*God sleeps in the stones,*
*breathes in the plants,*
*dreams in the animals and*
*awakes in the human being.*
Quotation from the Sufi tradition

Sitting in silence means
looking into
the silent sitting now
which sits there, as silently
as a sleeping stone.

Sitting in silence means
looking into
the breathing now
which breathes there, as silently
as a flower
or a tree.

Sitting in silence means
looking into
the dreaming and feeling now
which dreams and feels there, as silently
as a cat
or a small beetle.

Sitting in silence means
looking into
one's own looking,
so that this looking
may be woken up

by what it is looking at,
by feeling and dreaming,
by breathing,
by simply sitting in silence, here.

So that the looking
may wake up to the one
who sleeps like a stone,
breathes like a plant,
dreams like an animal.
Looks like an I.

## BROKEN

Sometimes, coming out of silence
you have an inkling of completeness.

Because of this inkling
you are, perhaps, again and again
all the more disappointed
that this completeness
does not persist as reality.

What is complete is whole.
Wholeness only manifests itself
by falling apart
and breaking into pieces.
Falling apart
is reality.

As soon as you take the broken as whole,
being yourself a part of the whole,
you sense and experience
in yourself,
and in every other part,
the one wholeness.

The whole reality
of the broken wholeness.

It is through complete acceptance
that the broken is
completely
whole,
in reality.

## TRANSFORMATION

When, occasionally, we get a sense
of the transformation
that comes about through practising,
we are always surprised.

For we hardly notice
the transformation itself.
It takes place
in the deepest layers
of our soul,
no matter
whether we feel good or not good
while we are practising.

Therefore it is not important
how we are while we practise today.
What is important
is that we stick with it.

## WHAT DOES IT BRING ABOUT?

Actually, you are still too tired.
Actually, you have no time today.
And what can this sitting in silence
possibly bring about?

What does it bring about anyway?
Does it bring anything about?
Does it bring?

Now that I am sitting here,
I might as well just bring myself.
Bring myself right into this silence.
Bring myself into this breath,
into this out and in.
Bring myself and myself.
Bring myself.

# SILENCE

## READY

Here I sit in silence.
Am I ready for silence?
Readiness is all.
Silence is grace.

## SILENT

I think
I should be silent.
Be silent
I think.
I think:
silent.
Silent
I think.
Silent.
I
silent.

## SCENT OF FLOWERS

How *can*
you silence
your senses?

This scent of flowers
which drifts in through the window!

There is nothing to be silenced.

Does not this scent itself
keep silent?

## AT THE EDGE OF THE ABYSS

Some people
believe
silence is found
somewhere
in paradise.

But real silence
is found
at the edge
of the abyss.

## WHOLE

Silence makes
each moment
whole.
Full.
Complete.

Silence also makes
pain
and suffering
whole.
Full.
Complete.

## THAT'S ENOUGH NOW

Deeper silence
usually comes
when you
have sat beyond
the threshold of
'That's enough now'.

When you
simply stayed put,
just when you wanted
to withdraw.

## ONLY THOUGHTS

Only thoughts today,
thoughts, over and over again,
and no trace
of silence.
I can do what I like.
Yet I cannot.
I cannot
not think.
I cannot.
That is how it is.
Doing becomes silent.
Wanting becomes silent.
I become silent
in the middle of
thoughts and
more thoughts.
Silent.

## ENLIGHTENMENT

I have been sitting
in silence
for so long –
and still
no enlightenment.

Now I am giving it up –
sitting for
enlightenment.

Now I only want to
sit
in silence.

Has it ever been
so silent?

## SILENCE IS NOT A MUST

Although silence is there, always and everywhere,
it does not appear
when you think
it is a must.

The secret of the practice is:
silence is not a must.

Silence is everywhere, always,
as soon as I stop thinking
silence is a must.

## FORGETTING YOURSELF

Listening to the silence.
Listening
until you forget your self
in the silence.

Forgetting yourself
into silence
until you wake up
as silence itself.

## THE DEEPER THE SILENCE

The deeper the silence,
the more do sounds
have a place in the silence.
Or, the other way round:
then silence dwells also
in all sounds.

The deeper the silence,
the sooner does walking
have a place in the silence.
Or, the other way round:
then silence itself is found
in your footsteps.

The deeper the silence,
the more often
the everyday also has a place in the silence.
Or, the other way round:
then silence is found
everywhere in the everyday.

Now,
in this sitting in silence,
you need not
concern yourself with it.
Now it is enough to notice
how the silence is deepening.

## UNDERSTANDING

When you sit in silence
nothing should interest you.
Nothing except nothing.

You may misunderstand this.

When you sit in silence
you need not understand.
Nothing except nothing.

# NOW

## INDESTRUCTIBLE

Whether I live or die,
It is completely
indestructible.

If I search for It,
I do not find It.

And yet It breathes
right now
silently
out and in.

## RIGHT NOW

When you look into
what is right now,
how it is,
and then check
how it came about
that it has turned out like this,
it may be that
you suddenly think
that this now
is nothing else
but the result
of yesterday,
of a long, long yesterday.

When you look into
what is becoming right now,
as it comes into being,
then you may get a sense
that the now
is also endlessly kindled
by tomorrow,
by a great, great tomorrow.

When you look into the now
until looking itself
melds with the now,
until you yourself
are nothing but now,
then it may dawn on you
how all that was and is becoming
is one whole,
an eternal present.
A single right-now.

## WHAT WAS IT?

All of a sudden
I sit here again
in silence.

What was it
in the meantime?
Was it me?
Now it breathes in.

## CENTRE

In the centre
of the now
there is no time.
No before,
nor after.
In this centre
now.

## COMING AND GOING

Being aware that you are sitting here.
Being aware how breath comes and goes.
Again and again – comes and goes.
Passes by and comes again.

There is no moment
in which breath stands still,
stays fixed,
stays now.

Going along with this movement,
this movement of
going and coming.

This is how you yourself come and go,
go and come,
just as
in this in and out
eternity itself
comes and goes
now after now.

## LIFETIME

All things pass quickly away.
The more of your life you have lived,
the more quickly it seems
to have passed.

What can you do
except not think about it?

Sometimes I imagine
I am a fly with a one-minute life span.

Then my only option
is to immerse myself fully
in this small now.

There is nothing there
which passes away quickly.
There, time is like eternity.
When you fully immerse yourself
in this immeasurably small now.

## THOUGHT

Yes, it may well be
that I have been thinking this and that
for quite a while.

But now
that I think that,
now
that too
disappears.

## THE PRESENT

It is breathing again.
Without my assistance
it breathes this flow.

I will not disturb
this flow,
not disturb it with my looking.

I will withdraw
behind my looking.

The more I retreat,
the more I myself am
nothing other
than this flow of breath.

The more I am not,
the more the present is.

## MOOD

You just come along,
not yet knowing
whether you are in the mood
to sit in silence,
but as soon as you sit
you find yourself
just there.

And you do not have to know
in what kind of mood
you have come.
It is enough
that you are now here.

## THE REAL THING

Many people follow
a thought pattern which says
that the real thing
will happen tomorrow,
or anyway later,
anyway not now.
This moment now
is, after all, far too insignificant
to count as the real one.

Clearly everyone knows,
that this is nonsense,
that the real thing
can only be now.

Do you truly know it?
Is the real thing happening to you now,
reading these words?
Simply reading this –
whatever it says.

Seeing these letters.
Seeing these lines,
the crooked and the straight.
This real thing.

## CLICK

It is true that
outwardly
more often than not
silence is
interrupted
by an occasional noise
from the street,
or by the sound
of a voice,
or by the click
of a door.

Sometimes
it is a disturbance.
Sometimes you do not hear it,
even though you hear it.

But once in a while
the disturbing sound
may unexpectedly turn out to be
what you have
actually
been waiting for.
A small click
that fulfils everything.

LIVING IT

Some people live
almost incessantly
in the conditional mode.
They would live, if.
Unconsciously they impose
conditions on life
before they live it.

The basic condition
we impose is
that it should be better.

If my life were better,
then I could live it.
If others behaved better towards me,
then I could live with them.
If I myself were better,
then I could live my self.

But right now life is not better.
Nor are the others.
And I too,
I am right now no better than I am.

Right now everything is as it is.
My only choice is
to accept it
or to fight against it.

However: no matter whether I accept it
or fight it,
right now I am living
just this life.
I cannot help
but live IT.
IT,
that large life, as my life.

Accepting is IT,
fighting is IT,
thinking about it is IT,
stopping thinking about it is IT,
silence is IT.

## NOT KNOWING

Just now it was
perfectly silent.
But
as I notice it,
it is
lost.

Noticing is
noisy.

Not noticing
is the practice.
Wide awake,
not noticing.

How?
The question is
noisy.
Not knowing
is the practice.

Not knowing.

# OBSTACLE AND SHADOW

## STORM

What storms have been raging outside
these past nights and days!
So how good,
to be able to stay inside,
at least every now and then,
inside the house,
and from this silent inner space,
simply to listen
to the power that is roaring and rampaging out there.

How great are the storms,
sometimes unexpectedly rough,
which break into the soul's landscape!

So how good
to be able to withdraw inside,
at least every now and then,
in order to dwell silently
in the inner depth of the soul
and listen
to the power
that guides even such storms.

In the middle of the storm,
how good
to dwell silently
in the inner depth of the soul,
breath after breath.

ENVY

Some people always think
others are better than they are.
No doubt other people
can even sit in silence
much better than they.

Others have long since
had no more pain in their knees or back.

No random thoughts,
let alone silly thoughts,
have ever occurred to others,
when sitting in silence.

Others have surely
made much more progress than they have.

Why are you not simply you,
the you who is sitting now?
Why are you not
incomparably you?

## AGREEING

Sometimes, although you are doing your best,
sometimes a pain comes anyway
and stays and even worsens.

Sometimes, although you are doing your best,
sometimes it happens
that all of a sudden you have had enough
of the pain which comes and stays,
although you are doing your best.

You can fight against it,
struggling within you.

Or you can recognise
that pains are there
and agree
that they are now part of you.

With your recognition
the pain calms down.
With your agreement
the pain feels
at peace with
millions of pains.

As if every single pain
were part of me
and sought peace
in this pain of mine.

## TIREDNESS

Tiredness is no obstacle
to sitting in silence,
but to think
tiredness is an obstacle,
that is an obstacle.

When you stop thinking this,
you can sit in silence very well
with tiredness,
however tired you are.

Then at last you are too tired
to get stressed
and to want to achieve anything.

Too tired,
to bully
your breath
and keep griping
about yourself.

Perhaps even too tired
to think.
Then the only thing to do
is to abandon yourself gently,
for this brief moment,
to the silence now.

## LIKE THE GRASS

Some people tend to
give up
if silence
will not come straight away.

I am no good at this.
There is really no point.

To bring yourself
out of this state of inertia
you can think of the grass
which, when flattened,
simply lifts itself up again
towards the light.

Silently
it lifts itself up
again,
because that is what it is meant to do.

If you do as the grass does
you soon find yourself
alert again
and in silence.

## CRAZE FOR MORE

Some people
always seek more.
Even if they
have experienced silence,
they seek: more.

Even if they
have experienced Now,
they seek: more.

More is a substitute for: whole.
The craze for more blurs
what was.

The craze for more destroys
what is real now.

The craze for more obstructs
what wants to come.

Whole is enough.

## ANGRY

No sooner has it become silent
than I get angry.
I would not have thought
that I was so angry.
That I am still angry.

Angry with this or that person
who recently
or a long time ago
hurt
or betrayed me.

I sit in silence
and would like above all
to take vengeance.

Really?
I stay here.
And hear how the silence says:
that is how it was.

I stay here.
And hear how the silence says:
this is how you are.

I stay here
with the silence.

## OLD PAIN

It has hardly grown silent
when there it is again,
the age-old
pain in my heart.

At long last
I want to stop feeling it.

Do not want it.
Do not want.
Not.
Nothing.
Want nothing.
Let go.
Feel.
Pain.
Yes.
Silence
around all
pain.

## ANNOYANCE

Just as it is growing silent
he comes into my mind:
this person
who annoyed me so much.

It is simply there, his image,
as if he wanted to sit here with me.
All right then.

I see him
while my breath
comes and goes.

My breath comes,
he is facing me,
my breath goes,
he is there.
Again and again.

I do not know
whether I then
forgot him –
or he me,
when just now
only silence was left.

But when I now
think of him
my breath knows:
reality is
quite different
from what I thought I was.

## WANDERING ATTENTION

Some people tend to
get cross with themselves
when they catch
their attention
wandering.

This distances them
from the silence
more than all the noise in the world.

But you can easily
stop being cross
merely by
listening once more
for the silence
and feeling in amazement:
silence does not get cross.

## WHAT REMAINS OF ME?

Some people fear
that silence dissolves everything.

Tension and cares,
oh yes, that would be good.

Thoughts and feelings,
oh yes, why not?

Concepts and distinctions
yes, yes, of course, yes.

But –
what remains of
me?

Fear is what
I am.

Fear,
until silence dissolves it
into one single
I.

## FEAR

I sit here and am afraid –
for her, for him,
for someone close to me.

I see what I fear in front of me.
See it,
see it,
see it silent,
see it silent.

See the feared thing
as if it had actually happened.

Already happened.
Idle to be afraid.

I sit there,
idle and carefree.
All at once I know:
what happens
happens.

## SEEING YOURSELF

Every time
thoughts
or feelings
distract you
from silence,
instead of pursuing the contents
of what you are thinking
or feeling,
you can
simply
see yourself in it.

See yourself think,
see yourself feel.
See only yourself.

Seeing is empty
of what
you see.

Seeing agrees.
Seeing sees:
that is how it is.

Silence is:
'that is how it is'.

## DISTRACTION

Here I sit and breathe
my breath silently.

But before long a distraction appears.
A ridiculous
tickle in my nose.
Should something so trivial distract me?
Yes, yes, it distracts.

A pain in the leg.
Oh, it is distracting.
A thought I did not even want to think.
A feeling I do not want to feel now.

Distraction comes unbidden.
You never want distraction.
But practice summons distraction
and practises by means of distraction.

So let us stop fighting distraction.
Let it come, welcome it.

Then it might happen
that by distracting,
distraction
points to something
that cannot be distracted.

Indestructible,
just now IT is breathing
this breath.

# SPECIAL TIME

## SPRING

Suddenly I see:
now is now
and now
and now.
Suddenly I see:
spring through and through.

## NATURE

When, after cloudy days,
you can at last
really enjoy
the sunshine again,
you marvel
at the beauty of nature –
the mountains, trees, flowers,
cows, beetles, butterflies!

Simply this nature.
This spontaneous being there,
this flowering,
this manifesting itself.

Do you know
that you yourself
are this nature?

Like the mountain, like the flower, like the cow –
spontaneous nature
just sitting here
ceaselessly manifesting itself
in this breath.

## WHITSUN

Sitting in silence means
letting images and concepts,
including images of God
and concepts of God,
depart
from our mind.

Sitting in silence means
letting silence be in us
and work within us,
until silence
goes forth
through us
into every encounter.

In this way,
without adding anything,
we can celebrate Whitsun
by sitting in silence.

## MIDSUMMER'S DAY

Today is midsummer's day.
While with this day
the height of summer
which draws us out of doors
is only just beginning,
the sun itself changes
its path, as if in secret,
and turns once again towards
the deep silence of the earth.

Perhaps this delicate tension
is at the heart of
the charm of summer.

Every morning
when we sit down with silence,
in a certain sense, we follow
the summer solstice.

While the bright day
which draws us out of doors
is only just beginning,
our consciousness changes
direction, as if in secret,
and turns towards
the deep silence of the night.

Preserving
this delicate tension
is then at the heart of
the charm of the day.

## ALL SOULS DAY

Today it seems to me
as though
all my beloved
dead
were sitting
at the walls
of my silent space.

## ADVENT

Already it is Advent.
As if you were taken by surprise.
As if the time
had passed too quickly.

Already it is Advent,
time which looks forward,
time for arriving,
so that Christmas
may not suddenly be
upon us.

Christmas
which will not become Christmas
if you yourself
have not arrived.

Already it is time to arrive,
in this sitting in silence,
in this breathing of mine,
continuously born
of the Single Breath
which, from moment to moment,
Advent after Advent,
christmasses
into this breath, now.

## NEW YEAR'S EVE

On the last evening of the year
You can mull over what has been:
what came off,
what you missed.

If you could think about everything
long and deeply enough
then you might well come
to acknowledge gratefully
that everything was
as it was.

When you now sit in silence,
it is not
in order to mull things over
but to let yourself enter
into the silence
of this moment,
to let yourself enter
so completely
that you are able
to acknowledge gratefully
that this moment
is
as it is.

## LAST DAY

Last day
here
in this place.

Not so!
Walking along the street
as always,
opening and shutting doors
as always,
sitting down and standing up again
as always.

As always:
only this one step,
only this door,
this sitting down,
this standing up,
this one time.

## ANNIVERSARY OF YOUR DEATH

I am sitting here,
miles
away
from your grave.

I am sitting here
today,
on the day you died.

And my breath
silently celebrates
you and you and you.

## THE WHOLE FEAST

The whole feast is over.
All the voices
have faded away.

Only the silence
is left.
Silence is itself
all the voices.

This breath
the whole feast.

# NEW DEPARTURES AND EVERYDAY LIFE

## EVERYDAY LIFE

To practise
in everyday life
in accordance with
an inner way
nothing is needed
other than quiet attention
directed at
what is going on
just now.

Walking.
Shaking hands.
Drinking water.

## CELEBRATING

We usually celebrate
after working hours or at a party,
not at work.

But why not celebrate everyday life?

Simply celebrate every moment
as if it were a party!

For a party it is enough
that friends are there.
They need not bring anything.

For the moment, too, it is enough
that we are there.

We need not bring anything.
Only be there.
To be there is to celebrate.

## THE STAIRCASE

What is practising for?
That the innermost nature of everything
may reveal itself to you.

Who shows it to us?
The vegetable,
the staircase,
the window.

Our eyes
do not see it.

But everybody has in them
that which can see IT.

## THIS CLOTH

My now is now.
This movement,
this getting hold of
and letting go.

This cloth,
this broom,
this pencil,
this keyboard key.

This key
that is my now.

## BEING MINDFUL OF SILENCE

If you are mindful of silence
during your routine work,
you come to respect
things
and people
more and more
as they are.

If you respect
people
and things
more and more
as they are,
then, very gradually,
you no longer
get quite so angry.

You can
leave it to your ears
to be mindful of silence.
Let your ears
listen out
for silence
while you
do your routine work
as usual.

## COMPLETELY FREE

Sometimes
when you stand up
after sitting in silence
standing up is
like sitting in silence.

Stepping along, too, is just like sitting;
everything is as though you were still
sitting in silence.

And yet,
with this step,
you are, more than ever,
completely
and wholly free
in any action.

MIRRORS

Sometimes
when you stand up
after sitting in silence
it is
as though you were facing
nothing but mirrors.

Whatever
I meet,
I see my eyes,
my face.

You and you
is me.
It and it,
pure me.

Mirrors of love
everywhere.

## FEET AND HANDS

When you
allow yourself to send some awareness
to your feet and hands,
then silence enters
of its own accord.

Through the silence in your feet and hands
you are suddenly present.

Forgetting yourself
in being present,
until you awake
in action.

## SUDDENLY

Suddenly
something makes
me pause
in the middle of the day.

Silence remembers.

And the next sound
is IT.

## FOOTPRINT

Emerging from silence
I go outside
only a few steps,
just for myself.

But all at once
my foot sees
how each step
leaves a footprint
and creates an effect.

So I never do anything
only for myself.

I go
outside,
just for myself.

# GUIDANCE ON PRACTICE

## ON POSTURE

As indicated in the introduction, an upright, well-balanced posture is conducive to sitting in silence. A straight backbone allows your breath to flow freely and helps to focus your mind.

Whatever sitting position you adopt, your knees should be lower than your pelvis, because if your knees rise above the upper pelvic rim, either your back is automatically crooked or it tenses up in order to keep an upright posture.

Your shoulders are relaxed and your head is tall, as if the crown of your head were being pulled slightly upwards by a fine thread, leaving your chin somewhat tucked in.
If you sit on a chair, it should be as firm as possible. The sitting surface should not tilt forwards or backwards. In order to keep your knees lower than your pelvis you may have to put a blanket or cushion onto the chair. It is best to put your feet at a natural distance apart and parallel to each other, with their soles completely flat on the ground.

If you sit on the ground on a cushion or on a rolled-up blanket, you cross your legs so that either one foot is in front of the other, or one foot is placed on the calf or thigh of the other leg. If you can do so easily, you can cross your legs so far that each foot rests on the thigh of the other leg and the soles of your feet face upwards (lotus position). Another possibility is to sit on your heels. In this position you can put a cushion or a blanket between your heels and your bottom to relieve the strain. Or you can sit on a low stool and put your feet pointing backwards between the sides of the stool, so that your toes face each other. This way your feet are not turned outwards, which could harm your hip joints.

For concentration it is helpful to lay your hands cupped inside each other (the left hand inside the right one) with the tips of your thumbs touching, so that an oval appears between your thumbs and first fingers. Your hands rest in contact with your body, with their sides one to two hand widths below your navel. Your arms form a rough circle so that your elbows do not touch your body.

It is best to keep your eyes slightly open so that you neither fix your gaze on a particular spot nor shut out the light in the room.

## PICTURING THE FLOW OF BREATH

Letting yourself arrive in contact with the ground
and in connection with the space above your head.
Finding a good balance between a gentle pressure
on the ground
and a slight pull upwards.

Allowing your attention to gather
in the space above your head.
Guiding your attention like a flowing movement
through your whole body;
that is, through the space of your head,
through the space of your neck,
through the space of your chest and shoulders,
through the space of your waist,
through the space of your abdomen
and also through your legs
down into the earth.

Allowing your attention to rise again
round the outside in a broad arc,
to the right and left of your body,
perhaps also behind and in front of your body,
allowing it to rise again to the space above your head,
from where it now flows down again
through your whole body into the earth.

When you have imagined this movement
and inwardly enacted it several times,
the flow of your breath will tend to link with it of its own
accord.

It is best when the inner downward flowing movement
joins with the out-breath,
and the outer rising movement
accompanies the in-breath.

So that the out-breath flows through your whole body,
as if from the space above your head
down into the earth,
to change there to in-breath
and as such to rise again round the outside.

After a while it may be
that in breathing out, the inner flowing movement
right through the body awakens an opposing energy
which at the same time tends upwards.
If it appears of its own accord,
this flowing counter tension
will naturally support
your upright posture.

In general the image of your breath may expand,
or become more detailed, or change.
But as simple a form as possible is the most favourable
for entering into silence.
For the only point
of this guided attention
is to be able to participate inwardly
in the process of your breathing.

The inspiration for this guidance came from working with Karl Metzler, mime and body work teacher, St. Ulrich near Freiburg.

The Oxford Zen Centre, founded in 1993, belongs to the Sanbo Kyodan school of Zen, a part of the world-wide Zen community. Its headquarters are in Kamakura, Japan but there are about 70 affiliated centres worldwide. In the UK weekly meetings are held in Oxford and London and longer retreats are also offered.

For further information and also additional copies of this book, please contact the Centre through its website at www.oxfordzencentre.org.uk

Living Silence is also available as an e-book.

The translators of this book are both practitioners at the Oxford Zen Centre.

Susanne Ehrhardt has published poems in English in magazines and anthologies, as well as in a full-length collection. Her mother tongue is German.

Wendy Tyndale has published articles and two books on religion and social issues, one on the Protestant Church in East Germany. She is a fluent German speaker.